What The Black Mirror Saw

– Stride –

By the same author:

WHAT THE BLACK MIRROR SAW

New Short Fiction and Prose Poetry

Peter Redgrove

WHAT THE BLACK MIRROR SAW
First edition 1997
© Peter Redgrove
All rights reserved
ISBN 1 900152 10 X

Cover photo © Ivan Sladek
Cover design by Wilf Whitty

Acknowledgements
Asylum, A Curious Architecture (Stride),
Grand Street, The London Magazine,
The Manhattan Review, Verse.

Published by
Stride Publications
11 Sylvan Road, Exeter
Devon EX4 6EW

INVESTMENT
SOUTH WEST ARTS

Contents

III. IN THE BLACK MIRROR

To P. Shuttle for sharing the
Mirror of the Giant with me, and to
A. Rimbaud for many concurrent Illuminations

'...a form of non-computerised virtual reality... Suddenly the page jumped from two to three dimensions... the way the world looks is the way I learned to see it... there are other ways of seeing the world, other dimensions right before our eyes... because the kind of concentration required to see stereogram shapes if a form of systematic relaxation, looking at the illustrations in this book is a kind of meditative practice...'

Foreword by Howard Rheingold to *Stereogram* (Boxtree, 1994)

'...the next step is to bring the guiding ideal images into the field of meditative vision and to maintain a purely contemplative attitude towards them, whereby the mere void of the initial state of consciousness is soon permeated with a peculiar activity. For now the image contemplated unfolds of its own accord, fanning out into a dream-like wealth of association; and the field that up to now was empty of intellectual and sensual association suddenly becomes charged with the energy of a magnetic field, pulling together, as though by a series of shocks, the associations belonging to the guiding image...'

Wilhelm Fränger, *The Millenium of Hieronymous Bosch*
(Hacker Art Books, N.Y. 1976), p.65

'Hold this postcard right up to your nose and very very slowly pull it away from your face. Look through the image without focussing on it. Try not to blink, and a hidden image will magically appear!'

Magic Eye Book of Postcards (N.E. Thing Enterprises, 1994)

'I have remarked... that if... the attention is energetically braced up to an act of steady observation... then if this intense condition of vigilance should suddenly relax, at that moment, any beautiful... object falling on the eyes, is carried to the heart with a power not known under other circumstances. Just now, my ear was placed upon the stretch, in order to catch any sound of wheels that might come down... the Keswick Road; at the very instant when I raised my head from the ground, at the very instant when the organs of attention were all at once relaxing from their tension, the bright star... fell suddenly upon my eye, with a sense of the infinite...'

Wordsworth in Thomas DeQuincey: *Reminiscences of the English Lake Poets*
(Dent 1961), p.122

I. HABITATIONS

WEATHERMAN

The shady shadowy man in shades she glimpsed from time to time; in every woman there lives one who is both father and bandit.

As that figure touched her mind, everything went wet with a heavy dew, including her own secret self; the air smelled of wet wool and steamy woodfires, and a cool air curled off the upper slopes of the hill, making mist.

Each time the weather changed and the great invisible humidities rolled off the estuaries on to the land, she expected to see the man coming round the corner of the house, like the visible herald of the invisible weather-change, or emerging from the bushes beside the stream and striding towards her, his dark glasses hiding the colour of his eyes, or with a hand held up to shade them as though she were some great light dazzling him, or for a disguise; but always arriving with an ambiguous and partly-concealed face, the clothes neutral grey, not quite frank in the face or in the dress, except for the body, which strode. Men stride, women walk.

He existed, all right; she had seen several of her friends talking to him, apparently without the apprehension she felt merely on seeing him; his arrival introduced a contrary weather, or did contrary weather induce him to arrive? The women were laying plates on the big tables on the lawn and they were talking as they did so, and the wind veered and became moist, and round the corner of the house he came, and though there was no pause in laying the tables, the conversations ceased until he had gone.

Once she mentioned the apparition of the man who came when the weather changed to one of her friends, one whom she had seen talking with him, and the friend stared at her in incomprehension; that was the one and only time she mentioned the occurrence to another.

'Perhaps, she said to herself, 'it is just a figure in my mind put there by some evolutionary force to unsettle my peace. He talks to others, and they will not admit it to me; when at last he speaks to me, will the others then acknowledge that they have seen him and heard him?'

SEX TALK

I.

Warm fog, small rain. This drizzle is not a depression, it is a distillation. Great condensations on the trees, whose trunks run like rivers. Then it is a vast rime; strong frost, bright and still fog. The hanging woods like universal fretwork. 'I will free your prisoners from the waterless pit.' Each tree-trunk a shiny brook distilled from its leaves and branches and, with the thaw, the whole wood a convocation of water-voices.

II.

That frigid day the swamp had turned to ice. Worms glassed in my footprint ice. Now the birds sing to the full moon in wormlight. Next morning: the sea moving from state to state, from choppy waveflame to full pulse, which flashing catches the sunlight, like Logoi splitting into dualities that continually join again. Because they are able to make love, she loves all people who share the communion of orgasm. Accordingly the flowers are raising their yoni-faces out of mud, partners for multitudes. I start to shave as the mists clear in the valley, like lips beyond lips that give kisses beyond touch.

III.

Sex pm. As I was kissing her left nipple, her skin turned oceanic; or it became like a tropical flower of immense dimensions, into which we were both inserted. We had only intended a short rest, with all glands tuned to the weather. But then there was equinoctial drainage. Suddenly noticed: a great perfume of outdoors, a discharge of clouds and rain like mile-high gates opening, revision of the glands, then the clouds re-building. We have come in accord with them, and they look as we feel.

APPLE AND BLACKBERRY

A little rural graveyard in which there are as many trees as graves. The graves have opened their windows, the coffin-wood has been raised into the bowers of the tree, whose branches are open to wind and sun; the gravestones the same colour as the moon – basic rock – are nearly consumed by orange lichen whose sensitivity to the air shows there is no pollution here. Birds sprint from one airy grave to another, like souls sharing space. A sparrow perches on the lip of a monumental angel. This graveyard is the best place for blackberries (ebony-sweet cluster fruit) along its misty paths; and for apples in the orchard which it adjoins; the green alembics in this cider-farm concentrate on distilling the sweet heavy drops in which the apple-seeds are suspended within a cylindrical core of five points, like a slice of a star-ray. Like the blackberry bushes, which raise the soil-dark into the sunshine where it sweetens and will produce a pure light in the mouth, the apple-trees are alchemists who are also their own apparatus, their crabby selves and the work itself; they are the Balsamos, the breeders of the airs and mists all around us. We human alchemists must re-learn our work here, out of doors. Someone has left at the church-door for the harvest festival a barrel of oysters grey as stones in ice; these grim gravestone oysters are reserved for the grown-ups; the children bring a cardboard box with a few apples and some blackberries reserved for God.

IN THE MARSHES

I.

The laughter of women picking blackberries together, the fruit loosening off the bush into the stained hand; seed, cushioned with nutrient; compacted, like a compound eye in a bird; tyre-tracks braid the mud as they cycle away, baskets full of berries still potent, the innumerable cobbled repast off the bines-stripped-green.

II.

He was a member of the expedition which found a mammoth in the peat-bog, its stomach packed with flowers and roots and stacked with camellia-petals like a leather-bound book; we slit the distended hide and petals (still bright and shining) slid out.

III.

He is walking between the sky-dykes, the reflecting puddles; they are like theories translated into wet dreams, from 'Yes, it will rain, I believe it,' to 'Come out into the rain, it's so warm'. He dips a toe into a puddle which shakes the world. We must improve masturbation's image, he thinks, the heavy tyre-tracks braiding into the distances, the sky running blue under the mud.

IV.

These are embraces: the women cramming blackberries through stained lips, the plaited tyre-tracks, the cargo of white petals flowing back into the world from the ripped belly of the antediluvian in the marsh, the reflective puddles dyked by the mud between them like bridges over or under the sky, the compound fruit that rejoices the women as much as the bowl mobbed with cherries, as much as a favourite timbre of massed cellos.

V.

The home in the deep marshes, now emptied of furniture; he walks over the hollow boards. As he drove towards the house he saw the grey sky reflected in its windows as though the house were full of sky, but it is not. There is a broken window which makes the whole place draughty. Wind clasps house, and passes through; he breathes a shuddering sigh, earth unclasps air. Air only, no sky. He breathes deeply, hoping that sky may enter his mind; sky, the comforter.

THE CONFERENCE

I heard approaching a faint unhurried voluminous rustle. It was the rising wind in the trees and also she, approaching over the lawn. She wore a grey-brown dress because, she said, white or pink frightens the birds. The gentlemen sat down in the long narrow room papered with gold but with a black ceiling – people talk best at oval tables. Still, she was a constant presence at the conference, since she was plainly visible to them on her low seat under a clump of double hollyhocks. The conference in the high, flat house behind its huge sycamore. Later, the members wandered in the garden and passed to and fro in the rambling orchard full of rose clouds of apples. She took papers and put them on the table's oval, like a person floating paper rafts on the watery shine of the wood, which deepened as the conversation took grip. Was she a house ghost? After the day's proceedings, the Chairman found her lying curled up in the bracken close to the driveway, so he almost trod on her, the colour of her dress hiding her, blending her with nature in her sleep.

EXPLANATION OF THE TOWN'S UNEASE

Whisking an omelette, mixing egg tempera, the same. On our palates we mingle the daily palette. Curtains are drawn, the model's throne set up, we pass the day in the red studio tasting her skin by palette in the process known as life-modelling. As the tongue is enthroned in the mouth, uttering, surrounded by her bone-headed artists.

Our practice is faulty today, due to farty technique from upset tubes squeezing. In this small resort there are simply not enough sewage-halls to accommodate the disjecta of the throngs of visitors. The artists of Rome set up their Venus Cloacina as figurehead in white marble, breasting the sulphureous torrents of the eternal city.

What creates that picturesque bolster-burst of gulls on the muddy flats? That is where a sewer debouches. The birds are also a flu-virus reservoir, and the virus is the second harvest that was used-up food. It is a ghost-food breeding in fevers communal dreams that slop loose sweats over the luxury sheets. It is a communicable mental illness of flu depression transmitted on the balms and wings of the breezy town, its 'fluence. For the greater part of the town's spirit-language is smells. Recall how the salmon sniffs from mid-ocean its birth-source out. The bonfire-burst of gulls, their winged breath... but the estuary is crowded also with the last breaths expanding through the casements of the Old Folks' Home; like a catafalque made of stone, gulls, doves hooting and sub-microscopic germs catalysing the tone of our paintings.

BREAD MEDICINE

Tearing into the new bread, buttering it as with a sword of sunshine, devouring the innumerable cells and mansions, belching the sweet smell of new bread, yes, it is an Antwerp of love constructed of innumerable mansions and all nutritious, and the crust crackling like wireless as you tear;

Even in this thunder-weather like wireless wolves snapping in packs; see how the wet packs blow from the wolf-coloured clouds;

Even when the women gather terrible poisons in their aching joints, which gather like thunder and flash at the eyes;

Even with Pasteur's Wood just outside, with each tree oozing a separate foetid gum which is a disease; these trees and women have no seed, only smells that fasten on the mind;

Except that one devours the new crust, he smells of clean yeast and crust and the fire-clean oven in which the bread glows and tans and still at this moment emits its sunshine invisibly in the energy of its smell; a radiant loafer, a loafer around that palace whose grounds and kitchens feed us all with root-mud and basic sunshine.

WHAT THE BEDROOM SMELT OF

The bedroom smelt of her babyhood. I say this – do I mean maidenhood, godhead, maidenhead, as Don Giovanni was said to smell out the maidenhead? I say again, the bedroom smelt of her babyhood. Thunder charged the perfumes. The world outside the window smelt thus also, of its maidenhead, its godhead, its babyhood. What was this coming, when godhead, maidenhood leaked like a perfume from where it had made its home? The perfumed chambers of every cell in the world: for, in health, aroma and fragrance; in disease, stench. To grow properly, they must smell of their babyhood. The weather reveals all these condensations as it turns.

YONIC COLLABORATORS

I.

Whenever you see a diamond, suspect a Yoni. Dia-mond – Goddess of the World. The Yonic shrine or diamond seat. Clambering into the diamond-shaped yoni of the world on the side of the mountain. To sit there like the man in the gate, meditating. The Thomas Gray meditation, as in Shuttle's story. The rain descends from above, where the fixed star is. It smells of the sow, and that is good. The pillars of the door are anointed with their various self-generated unguents, and there is a small puddle of blood into which one lower's one bottom, in which one sits. My Yoni paddles in my chest, resumes its beat. I am in position, the thunder may arrive. Thunder can dissolve diamonds, in the sense that when the thunder peals, the pillars stream with juice, the secret door widens its Iris on the corridor behind. It is my cue to climb in further. Diamonds are sexual, and can bring forth children like themselves, and I see one of them shining on my lover's brow.

II.

The people are meditating, and sit straight in their own perfume, which gives them the sheen to their thoughts. When she walks into a room, its gender changes. A cloud of the right kind hovering over a head makes the person shine beautifully. This meditator is up to his waist in the sea, like a kind of centaur. A great lion-chested man considering how the lake boils with whitecaps as the lightning strikes it.

THE WOMEN SPIN

I.

He was a great chymist and studied most in his sea-voyages.

II.

Nude wine all drunk up, bare wine, stripped of its bottle, flesh of wine working all naked within me.

III.

The god in his vaults possessed the child in her womb, speaking in a belly-voice or ventriloquism.

IV.

The altar of the dressing-table where the female sacrament is confected. Prams repainted in tender colours. The kiss over the cradle made them both dizzy. The baby's radiance made them kiss. He was the golden battery.

V.

Standing on the garden path, watching the thunderhulks reflected in the windows, as if the thunder like burglars had broken into the house.

VI.

Silk-cocoons shining on the sill like angel-turds of finest silk. The rain water-barnacling the windows.

VII.

What does it mean, to say 'The women spin'? They sit there, talking, turning, spinning yarn very slowly – it is their pleasure; then suddenly they reverse and spin fast the opposite way, sending out a strong breeze, like the coloured breeze of a musical top.

THUNDER-FACTORY

A splash of ice across a mirror. Ice on a silver button. The frozen waterfall, a construction of cavernous glass tents with hitched-up doorways, the structure of the falls revealed as in a solid high-speed photograph. The many clouds become one cloud which shakes its head over the mountains and grazes the lowland dormitories. In the thunder-factory's vast white sheds thunder echoing creates sleep; as the thunder-echo dwindles you are carried out of your body to sleep. The cistern cracks, and water flows over grass, the women splash through the thin watery sheets, for fun, barefoot. They come out of that cloud in their snowy dresses, out of the waterfall's tents, out of the white-furred fountains and out of the thundering halls of mirrors and torrents circulating in the high air, buoyed up by their great skirts, rotating serenely downwards like the keys of a white ash. The full moon breaks the clouds, and stretches out into the air its arms of air.

GRANITE GAZING

Granite cannot burn; it transforms. As the lava pushes through the stone gates, the granite of them, encountering the vehement temperatures, projects a metamorphic aureole, like a rainbowing bruise of its body. Our county is made of this aureole of rocks. The primal granite is like the bones of God which quake to the movement of stars. You can see the stars glittering in the stone; it is an observatory. But the creatory of the mother accords more easily, and it was for this reason that the deities entered the human womb, that is, for easier breathing, of a more competent amplitude, and not plunged into the womb of rock that gives only one hundreth of a millimetre to the passage of the moon. Now the harmonious beating of the hearts of mother and child accord. She raises her sail, like big-bellied Isis. She raises her soul, and the granite cliffs begin to flow. She carries the child lightly, and thus, with a simple movement, such as this raising of her sail, can move the world in its entirety.

TREE AND HOUSE

The mid-spring garden of a shuttered house. At the ponds the child points out insects coupling. In the walled garden how delicate a deep but airy flower seemed to her. A cloud spins a perfectly-round shadow across the lawn and there is a sudden heavy shower. The child stands there, amazed, soaked through, pointing at the dragonflies that are still coupling in the air which is full of raindrops. The rain does not strike them, they shift only slightly. The rain is too delicious to desert. The house's white facade shakes bright against the steady leaden cloud-banks and resembles a portico into the cloud. She shelters in the rain-shadow of a large slanted yew. She climbs up as far as she can among the needles and is in the rain's house which is quite dry inside; she imagines coupling with her soul's mate here.

A MENTAL LIGHT

A mental light is seen across the estuary. A woman eats the last mud-fish. Inside the house, you are outside the wind and rain. Outside, you are inside them. As with roses, what outside can match this inside? She built a God's corner in her house in the Russian manner. The Great Warrior wishes to rest in the Moist Cave, and so she makes a God's Corner in the feminine manner. It is as though there is a small red carpet laid down to honour his penis, and all pomp and circumstance has been fulfilled, and there is silence. Now it is that she sees the mental light flash across the estuary. Now it is that she eats the last mud-fish, as he sleeps.

BRIEF VISIT TO MALVERN

Wooded Silurian limestone ridges separated by a vale of softer shales suitable for pasture. The 'toposcope' set up on a Malvern peak draws a postcard into the eye with a snatch of music. Elgarscope. At the foot of the hill, one of the great spa hotels spreads. It is haunted by the ghosts of Malvern water; drinking the water gives it legs and you health; it is a pleasant two-way deal; now the halls of relaxation are fretted with woodworm, always on the job. Malvern Water – Langland drank it, slept and saw – we drink it out of each other's hands – she rubbed a little on her bosom and immediately it became the milk of the breasty hills – 'out of that famous hill / There daily springs / A water, passing still.' The station built in cast iron remains; the locomotive sparks would have torched a wooden one or sintered away a stone one as by continued fusillades of bullets. We paid our ticket and walked out into the railway theatre. There was a Link Stone, a Whore or Hoar Stone, a boundary marker, coins were placed in its moist cleft as payment for crossing the boundary; and she was so much recovered by the waters she could see the flea hopping on my pillow.

OYSTERS AND GRAVEYARDS

I.

Like the graves, these oysters are something between stone and beast. The graveyards of oyster-coloured stone fill with autumn flowers, brought by survivors moving as slow as oysters. As a dreamer might see the remnants of his dream projected on the ceiling above his head, the dead devise their fantasies among their secret boxes of tars and tattered skin, project their images above the soil of themselves in the form of a garden-plot – in this place a face of flowers has formed by apparent accident, and a green body with hands clasped over the chest lies quietly with a small green Christmas tree for an erection. The wind gently massages the cones of this sensitive tree, and its spiny face beams widely and lets out puffs of yellow pollen.

II.

What of the oysters then? They are a different mystery. Despite the resemblance to gravestones of their calcareous houses, each is shaped like a woman's purse. Their enigma is a muscular phlegm whose fringe or arch is studded with sky-blue eyes. I look up into the sky, matching it with the constellation 'Arch', as if an angel were standing up there in the West, watching us with a band of stars. Oysters do however resemble the graveyards in this: at certain times they open wide and feed, the estuary water streaming through their watchtower arches.

ARRIVAL

Electricity creaks in the clouds. MacDonald's Golden Pillars arrive in the high street. As the dew clears from Dingle's window we see that lobsterback uniforms and shirts with furbelowed sleeves are *de rigeur*. As the people march and countermarch on the early morning meadow we see they are clothed thus as gorgeous infantry which bursts out of the mist into the cold bright sun, and marches back again and disappears into the mist as into the smoke of cannons. A doctor is there who has to unlearn his training; he must kill. A hidden ivory man comes out of his closet, and streaks through the ranks in the oldest uniform of all. The two lovers make it up, marching and countermarching through each other and are able to forget the unpleasant shape of the hotel room that comes to a point in the southern corner.

SKYDOLLIES

From *Idol* we get the word *Dolly*. In the fat grip of the wind a cloud-dolly rears its head and you can smell its landscape-scent as it stretches its skull, bursting all over with masks of God. We must bow the head and await the voice – less for its message than for relief after utterance; all its prophets wear similar beards and bardic hair. The Idol continues to rear up its cloudy miles moulded by invisibles; its oracular caves are burrowed out by the Jet Winds.

We are commanded not to make images, but you cannot stop the sky flowing. I see W.G. Grace in cricketing flannels trudge over the horizon, bend, and kiss me goodnight with a little rain. Out of his thunder-coloured cheeks the shining wool-beard spins, and he never looks like the same dolly twice. Are these eyebrows moustaches, are these eyes open or shut?

UNGARETTI'S FIREPLACE

I.

We walk in search of the coal and wood fire lighted every sunset at the Inn. We walk there in the frost of the evening under stars nailed to the sky by the frost and stars of frost underfoot nailed to the road. Our harsh skins grow thirsty for the fire's warmth, as if our pelts were the drinkers, walking us like dogs to the pub. As we enter it the air which enfolds us is spicy and relaxing like an atmospheric punch. We shed our coats, and drink juices. I read Ungaretti, needing guidance from the poet.

II.

In taking this walk it seems to me that I am stepping out of my frosty chains. By becoming cold under the hammering stars I have prepared myself for the presence of the fire which releases me. We pass from the frigid antechamber in the fire-lit bar. In that cave of Plato it was a fire lighted behind their gyved heads which projected the shadows the pinioned viewers took for reality. Now I am seeing the fire with my skin as well as my eyes and I understand Plato's fire is also this one made of contemporary wood and ancient coal, wherever it is laid.

III.

An actual fire creates an actual room, though it may also project shadows. The fire has its shadows within, its smokes, its loopholes of further brightness, but these are not its being, nor could we stroll unharmed through its radiant caverns, except by reverie. It is that the fire's processes total a reality, communicated to us by the touch of its warm smell and by its vibrant atmosphere, by sensation-thought. Thus our skins seem suppled into touch which is almost sight, and which modulates sight. Not the fire. The fire-in-the-hearth.

IV.

The stars are sharper yet as we return along the frosty road. The moon is set in pearl of itself, like a pearl in mother-of-pearl, which is the round moonbow of the frost. The houses on the way are brimming with light, they are full and overflowing. The tower on the point revolves its twin beams which reach like Newtonian callipers over the sea, like cartographer's fire measuring out the dangers.

SLOWLY AS A NAIL GROWS

I.

In the geological museum of the school of mines it was as though the ground underfoot was penetrated by the pipes of a vast organ that almost inaudibly played the theme 'descend, descend' arousing an appetite like a taste in the mouth to descend. Or was it like a great ocean-liner with its staircases and galleries lodged in a subterranean abyss, this mining-place, with ports open to the stone seascape, ready to cruise through the strata like a sunken moon? Then we were told that people under 18 were not allowed to Descend, and this meant that Z could not come with us. So we elected to stay above ground, this year anyway.

II.

I tried to interest Z in the specimens, the case after case of dusty rocks bearing amazing but undescriptive geological titles, and neither she nor I could summon up much magic. But then P swam around the corner with the air of a person who has been reading a profoundly absorbing book, and with a smile told me in a low voice that 'the crustal plates on which the continents float drift as slowly as a toenail grows...' When I touched her hand simply to thank her, all the dull rocks in their cases became jewels, each one in its correct place and faintly singing like the rigging of a great stone ship.

III.

I suppose it is a fairly common experience in a depressive that his turn towards mania will take graphic form: my ghost pushed through the sutures of my skull and escaped into the upper air, where it gave a great sigh and expanded into the sails and spars, hull and rigging of an adventure-ship. These sails shone like an astronaut's foil, and as the sun rose with the new moon in its arms, the pressure of the light from these orbs stirred my ship until it was scudding at full speed into the darkness – and the darkness receded because my sails were carrying large scale reflections of sun-with-moon in varying modes like a reflecting telescope with many kinds of mirror – the outspreading convex and the deeply-magnifying-like-a-shaving-mirror, the concave; my holds full of spices, olbanum, myrrh, cassia, and the perfume rising from these holds was an intricate part of the rigging.

Then there was Bentalls department store to visit. Even on the sunniest days it was brighter indoors there. There was an entrance opening by electric eye, a bronze door self-opening into the regions of soft music and special offers. There was a grand concourse with stairs that were also self-operating, climbing, descending. In the theatrical space between these escalators there might be a painted galleon heaving its way through a cotton-wool sea; or a Father Christmas drawn by reindeers with electrical bulbs fastened to their harness, in his sled full of parcels made up exactly as the counter-assistant would wrap your purchase, in cubical or rhomboidal shapes, very straight-edged and with festive paper; or, out of season, phalanxes of men's suits worn by moustached wax dummies with Brylcreem hair; or a Royal Ball with Cinderella in a dress white as the floorwalker's shirt but with flashing sequins all over. To look at anything in this shop was to join the multi-media show, to touch, taste, smell.

Once when I was crowding knee-high among the grown-ups some man's cigarette burned the back of my hand and I cried out for my mother. All the pale faces turned down and looked at me with mouths at O, and she took me then by my unburnt hand to the drapery counter where I forgot the insult and pain as the great pillars of fabric were flung down and unrolled as they travelled along the long polished bowling-alley of a counter with the inch-rulers screwed along its length, in a sudden blaze of light and colour like immense electrical shirting which crackled and blazed.

Once in later life it happened that I got very drunk in Leeds, and could not remember plainly where I had been; only I had a recollection of wandering through a store of great rolls of brocade and draperies that were unrolled for me and in which I dressed, turning around in such yards of material that my robes filled the warehouse. I asked one of the friends who had started out with me whether or not we had burgled the warehouse of one of the great Leeds cloth factories. Without a word he took me down the street and up the lino stairs to the little room under the eaves where I had passed out, a music student's bedsitter. I recognised it but knew at the same time that one of these walls had opened to admit me to the wonderful experience of woven and brightly-coloured stuffs, illuminated by a light that was Bentalls' light. Against this wall stood a radiogram. My friend put a record on, and I realised as the music unwound that this had been the cloth, and the record was the bolt on which it was wrapped. I had passed out and not merely heard the music, but was wound in it so that I touched and saw it too. That was the first time I had heard Verdi's *Requiem*.

MANUDUCTION

I.

The morning air sharp as reverse ether, that de-anaesthetises. Open shirt to open blouse – two lilies harkening to each other. The pollen of the chest, the balsam on the bosom, the bosom-friends. The opening at the throat like the heart's white ear-trumpet. The frenulum of the garment, its little bridle where the cloth fastens, in him, left over right, in her, right over left. I am the only one afraid of these matters. However, this is what we see, as a preliminary to exchanging fluids in the name of God.

II.

A sculpture parkland sited on a Cornish cliff. 'It was the great place you read about in books.'

III.

The rock she picked up was sparkling with musicals, it glittered like theatre curtains, it was a heavy tassel of the theatre.

IV.

Entering by mistake the Ladies: waterhiss, a pleasant tang of colognes, a carpet on the floor, two vases of fresh flowers and six small confessionals.

V.

The clouds hiss as they cross the view. They contain various transcendentals eager to drop on the visitor sheltering beneath the pines.

VI.

Honest, rational clothing, dispensable. The lovebites like a ring o'roses.

IN INSECT

I.

Gossamer from twig to twig shoots flashing rays – spider-fire. In the varying winds a shining cloth, spiderhouse with rope walls, sailing vessel, its stretched sails cast the shadow of a ghost-ship on which the dry husks take their voyage. A deep tablecloth of floss, of many storeys, a tablecloth of feast, of scoured utensils.

II.

The huge live oak that shelters the hot springs, the coils of steam caught in the boughs like the hanging carcasses of dragons who have been copulating until they are white, and mist only, white dragons flopping over the boughs transiently in long gobbets, converted entirely to seed; beware its touch, maidens.

III.

The white grandfather clock celebrating in its trunk dark conjunctions.

IV.

A kind of felty or furry yellow fly – call it an Orange Bonker – that feasts and copulates expeditiously in the broad storeys of cowparsley and its curds of pollen. Others with long shiny bodies like low-slung motorcars, in the still day the antennae waving as in a high wind. This is the way to shout across the banquet-flowers in Insect – Hey! Big Woman Longbright!

MIRROR WORKSHOP

I draw the milky nets of your negligence into my mirror-workshop. Veteran saturday-armchairs thrown out for the children and dustmen. Since she was wearing rather delicious black gloves up to the elbow, he introduced himself immediately. Pansy found that the glow she held in her skin from the cold douche room set off the gloves exactly. So did his attentions. Her hair was a lovely yellow, like amber burning softly. Fruit sweet as my salvation. Cautiously I lifted the lid of the box – midwinter silks.

WRITTEN LIMESTONE

The May-smell needs to be diluted by the wind. Then it is earth-shaking.

The dried dung balls clinging to its thick wool click like castanets as the startled sheep sprints away from us.

The Priory arches like standing waves of a silent organ music; the gigantic labour of the trees piled up in leaves, their towers.

The blossom on the May heavy as ice-cream; a wild world of limestone-writing, the stone nibs of the stalactites, the thousand-year-old stone flowers, the always breath-sound or mantra of the caves, with here and there a stone etched with the imprint of a sleeper who has got up, a pilgrim who slept darkness-pavilions around him.

II. PERSONAGES

THE SENIORS

I.

The two Seniors usher me into the stone circle. They inform me that the rocks are veiled masters, who have achieved a mineral trance by tuning in to their own crystalline bone-structure. A mind-picture slips into my head of an Old Master scratching his bald head with his chalky fingers until at one spot the voices come through, like a crystal radio with its catswhisker.

II.

Each elongated stone acts as a macromicroscope piercing the earth and surveying the stars underground, which are the reflections in the subterranean strata, in the great mirror-substance of the globe, of the stars above. I walk up to a stone and apply an eye to it. 'That is not the way,' say the Seniors. We pause under the lintel at the entrance and look back into the circle. 'Regard the dew,' say the Seniors, 'which reflects in its constellations the stars underground.' They lean on their staffs. I am open-mouthed. It is a perfect astrolabe, marked with the track of our plashy footprints.

III.

The two Seniors are called Drs. Silence and Taverner. They have their differences. Silence believes that minerals are entranced, plants asleep, animals dreaming and humans awake. Taverner believes that humans are asleep, animals awake, that plants invent and minerals contemplate. Both say to me that I must not believe everything the other tells me. Neither comes to abuse or blows – they are Seniors. Both like to have their own way. Both do much good in that way.

IV.

The Doctors differ too in their attitude to sex. Silence keeps his semen padlocked up as in a cage, like a confidential albino gorilla studded with blue sparkling eyes. He lets it out for exercise only at long intervals. Taverner pours his semen copiously on his brain's brazier by injaculation or retroactive masturbation, where it explodes into highly-coloured manias. I believe that their own fragrances of personality are wrongly overmastered by the example of their predecessors, the stone astronomers, whom they automatically refer to as 'men'. It is the natural assumption of the two Seniors that their superiors were once very much like themselves. The observatories of their handsome unlined countenances are serious porticoes with generous entrances housing perfect instruments, tribute in flesh and bone to their dedicated lives. Accordingly, as the others did, they will join the circle in their millennial state as the selfless star-gazing petrifacts contemplating the fresh emission of the stars nightly.

V.

I myself would prefer that the semen of the two Seniors were dedicated differently: to the anointing of Mrs. T's Nothing and the oiling of the portals of the Mistress of Silence. As matters turned out, that delightful double discipline was left to me, and I became apprentice to the women, while keeping the old fellows in good humour by listening attentively to what they had to say, and showing appropriate astonishment. The latter was not feigned, for I gradually gained the women's knowledge by sleeping with them, and was able to marvel at more than one version of the truth.

WATER CINEMA

She steps off the scrubbed deck where canvas whitens the light, steps out of the echo of canvas where voices are magnified in a cavern of winds, steps down from the rainbow-pavilions thrown from the tide on to the acres of white sail, water-cinema of the rainbow-fleet; thus she fills the saloon bar by the act of herself; as the sailing ships shadow the cool harbour in their aura of tar, brass, paint and pink gin, so she fills the local with her atmosphere and weather.

Her companions are three black men who step into the sunlight out of the white climate of the sail and the bleached planks like the sharp-edged shadows haunting her full-sailed blouse; whereas she is more than visible in shadow and sunlight, they appear, and disappear back into the shadows, and step out again, black brightwork, handsome for her.

She comes ashore wearing black boots and spumy frills: I see a moving surface of sails, surf and buoys like a portrait of the town shadowed in fold and crease across her fine linen, sailing her to the bar.

In her hold is her secret sharer, her hold is weighted with a salty cargo, a young sailor on his trapeze of dusky round waters within his harbourage of dome and sphered walls, and she adds by her potations strong waters to her baby's drink: as the sweet bubbles froth out of her drink or potion, so her commanders wink and laugh by her side in their black skins and gold teeth like brightwork; bubbles so weird and softly-pleading to her lips.

Her commanders quaffed the fresh young wine of her presses, and the youngest commander of all is everybody's hue; she calls for drinks all round including her baby's, she shares her wine with all the sailors there, black or white, born and unborn; she munches a cube of bright cheese: it is bewitched to flesh and blood in that nave; he floats under the ivory masts to the rhythmic drumbeats, he has nothing to do except listen to her body-music and her voice above muffled like wind in sails, 'The same again, please!', and sample the waters which are on the house.

Her ogive lace is like navigation of the spume; surely it is charts of her insides for when he leaves home. Meanwhile she voyages in the spindrift of these clothes on her own white decks under her lancet canvasses and cruciform masts, her sails all big in the belly and the breeze carries them away, she sipping warm red wine with her baby in the cup, chatting up her black commanders whose gold buttons are spermatic, every stud.

ESSAY ON THE CARDINAL

Flies in his presence that seem dressed in stainless steel. There are scents which rise and others that fall. Under the chateau d'eau the quiet man blew his groceries. Chateau d'eau: watertower; undertaking: the quiet trade; blowing his groceries: vomiting. Actually he was a smartass assistant prof blueskying his way. The blue sky gathers darkness, grain by grain, presto-magesto. They slept together in the Russet Room, with the bronze sheen like an apple in the wallpaper. The cardinal had flown off for another month. Their affair did not terminate with his Eminence's return. He seemed to carry with him pockets of clear-air electricity, and unexpected results. Fucking the pregnant woman, he impregnated her child too, so she was born pregnant. In another case, his son impregnated his mother from the womb, so that when he was born, she was still pregnant with his daughter, the cardinal's grandchild. He was a man of trick bookcases. He gaveth his beloved sleep. From his study in the old chateau d'eau he watched the smartass professor blowing his groceries. The trees stood unrespiring, holding their breath. A mystery is like a wheel, or a cardinal's hat. The hub shapes it. As the hat rolls towards you or rolls away, all you can see is the brim turning round and round the still crown. I saw the woman like a white flame in her nightdress hurrying with eyes bolting through the haunted gallery. I did not then know the scarlet nub of the trouble. Why should they dress in scarlet? The row of great wheel-like hats with their hubs full of head nodded and conversed. Did all these eminences possess our cardinal's secret? Or was there no secret, merely that they were depressed, and all the other people in their lives rushed around and were the occasions of strange happenings to compensate? A smell like blood and ozone on his breath as he kissed.

RASPUTIN

Rasputin, to get self-assurance, pushed his hand into his shirt and vigorously rubbed his left nipple, progressed round to his armpit, rubbed his hand in that, brought the hand out and sniffed it, then began to pray. As he prayed, they united happily in the dark in a faraway castle; their magnetic oils mingled and rejoiced; they enfolded into each other. Rasputin sighed, and got up off his knees, and spat through the window. The tall cumulo-nimbi were approaching from the distance. They were storing power as they travelled, by draining it from the landscape over which they passed; they were robbing the land, these tall white thieves with their blackening masks. As they passed over his head, they would rob Rasputin of his spirit. They would drain it from the white parting down the middle of his shining black hair and carry it away over the housetops and drop it elsewhere bestowing it on whom? Maybe those who united happily in a faraway castle. But a sniff of his breast would put Rasputin right. There would be a high-pressure system moving in after this cold front, and there would be energy in plenty to draw upon then with his prayers. Low pressure sucked up energy, high pressure fountains bestowed it. Between the two, the frigid and the calid fronts, sailed whitechalk cliffs splashed with inky torrents, passed silver-plated vacuums overhead, and the latter would dip down and sip from Rasputin's skull like a snake drinking brandy. How he loved the brandy of a thunderstorm when the great casks had split and the spirit lay around in puddles everywhere diffusing bouquet of its travels and the alcohol of great heights! 'This water has fallen two miles, gathering speed like runaway express trains which were all dining-room full of vodka,' says Rasputin, licking his lips.

DR. MORIARTY

The gun smelled of cordite and hot oil. It was in the hand of the man with a face like a run-over hedgehog. Curls of hair sprouted from within his collar like flames. He was called The Professor. He had started dark rumours about himself to promote his resignation from the department. His favourite tipple was the Beaune of a comet year. This personal shooting was a unique event, for the truly great criminal remains unknown; his heads are not killed, they merely float free of him, like natural events, time passing. No one points the finger. One could only assume his patience was finished. Duly impressed by his dark aura, the jarvey cracked his whip. We were so astonished that Holmes was still standing that we let Moriarty pass. There was a splash of smoke on the great detective's shirt front, that was all the outward sign. But the shock had robbed him of his voice. I hated this kind of childish mind-prank. Moriarty used the city as if it were a machine he had personally designed. Today, forty years later, a slight spookism made me reluctant to go upstairs, as though Moriarty was visiting.

GETTING OUR ROCKS OFF

All was cemented by a wonderful Perranporth walk. She held me in a certain grip until my rock-dark within shot up the spectrum and marbled like oil on water (or children's marbles rolling on granite pavements glittering with quartz or the closed pages of magnificent ledgers). This marbling flowed naturally into her until the doors between us disappeared and our inner gardens were furnished with tapestry of the one texture. This enabled us to see the broken-open surfaces of stone around us in the cliffs and in the personal pebbles which she held – it was a textured tapestry of that place, no sooner seen than touched, and, in her gesture, no sooner touched than seen. I could hear the Cleave Horse in the Stable of Slate making ready, saddling for his morning's gallop. In that case all answered to the motif 'horse' in the sea's manes, the headland face of a horse lying with its cheek in the water, the clouds like the breath of horses on a cold day expanding their changeable fractals of steeds and, galloping over the tussock land, the shadows of steeds; and ourselves riding in a manner which cannot say who is the rider and who the horse, nor needs to.

DR. MAGISTER CHILDHOOD

Arise and join them, was her motto. Gradually putting heaven together. The noiseless scarlet slippers which are called sanctuary shoes. Dr. Magister said he has heard a sound in the sky like a proposal of thunder: 'Will you marry me?' it said, in tones too deep for decipherment. The flat reminded her of an antique helmet, big enough to walk into: Goliath Mansions. These were plausabilia, almost pseudologia. Sheep among the vines, small white clouds flocking on the slopes of the gathering thunder. She opened a window of the helmet, a visor, and heard the landscape rustling. Light, and the machinery of light, as in the cinema, shafts and blades of picturing. Light and the light shed by stone. A French horn was playing a gallop and with the music came the pigs' fresh sweet stench. Gradually putting heaven together; I was ill then, but now I feel I need to be forgiven, visiting my early haunts in the guise of a girl-child. Have mercy, and to spare. He stared at miracle until it formed itself into a system, with which he housed and clothed us. His presence was like a candle alight, just the atmosphere around him, it refreshed me, the visit altered all that could be perceived.

SOMEBODY LENT IT TO ME

A shack by a creek of black mud and rotting trees is Count Fathom's Dazzle House, occupied by the person who has furnished this creekside cottage with chairs and seableached tables and pieces of bed washed up by the tide. An apple eaten by moonlight was as black as the mud – a deep and dazzling darkness – but tasted of glory. The somebody lent me this shack after we had united happily in the dark mud, or was it in the dark bed? My new friend took a nightdress, a pair of slippers and a bible from her suitcase, and arranged them neatly on her side of the bed. Was there a place here for her black fiery pearls, tiffanies of sperm, secret and famous lunaria? She returned many years later, and gave her own account: he opened the gate that led into the forest with the cottage by the creek. Even here it was hot. My period had come and I did not know whether to be pleased or angry. It was an old woman who unlocked the door and led me into a beautiful garden. I looked around for the creek of black love, I mean mud. I saw its shape around me, but it was blooming with roses on the south-facing bank, rosebushes with walks of black soil between them, and the smell of the mud transmuted through their glowing trumpets to a higher balsamic chord. The shack was still there, half-concealed by greenery. The tide came up to its threshold and the plain silver fish tattooed by the restless waters nibbled at the weed on the wood. The storm broke – we retired under the arbour. 'Out in the storm, all wet, like running through mirror after mirror, there goes the wizard's own boy,' remarked the old woman.

A KIND SMELL

I.

John says that he does not know the answer himself – 'Nor have I heard about it, except from you.' The one who seeks the truth is also the one who reveals it. John says, 'Do not tell lies, and do not do what you hate.' He may become the disciple of his own mind. 'If you do acquire a friend, do not entrust yourself to him. Entrust yourself to God,' and again, 'Whoever perceives divine reality becomes what he sees. Whoever has not known himself has known nothing, but he who has known himself has at the same time achieved knowledge about the depths of all things.' Do you want us to fast? How shall we pray? Shall we give alms? What diet shall we observe?

II.

After I had set myself straight, I saw the perfect child. I saw a Jesusa in white clothes talking and walking hand in hand with some men and some children. There was a stillness of silence within me, and I heard the blessedness whereby I knew myself.

III.

A child in stumbling across a room for the first time receives a deeper impression than his elders would from a visit to Italy. A child who realises for the first time that the person with the kind smile over there is his mother is more completely gripped by his emotion than the husband who leads his bride home. A kind smell.

BEQUEST

The gibbous moon under a heavy load. The small perfumed bones like pencils. They might have been good friends if they hadn't been husband and wife. The reek of the smouldering pot. Debating sleights, debating slaughter. At that hour the ashes would be mingled of husband and wife. The undertaker dreaded the laying-out of his father, he was half-awake, sobbing, only to be soothed back to sleep by the girl at his side; his mother's ashes had waited eleven years for the mingling. Death's house, its etiquette was perfect. Afterwards, her hand in her mother's hand, listening to the women debating murder. The corpse said 'Thank you. I have no further need of you.' The living persons, each of whom is only his own thought. In contrast, the undertaker's woman converted into a wonderful kitchen with all its gas-rings working; this kitchen is edible and functions at full strength during the wake; it is hung with food from wall to wall.

PARASYN NEXT STOP

The railway officer was drinking dry coffee-powder from a silver-plated mug as we waited in the flagstone passageway for the train to come in. Eventually it arrived, pouring so much steam upwards that it was as if it wished to turn entirely into a high-velocity cloud. The woman's perfume fitted her perfectly. It was jasmine, and unwinterish. They arrived at Clear Lake House, and settled in. He worked his hounds in the fresh snow. She exhaled into him. He was brilliantined as shiny and black as a tadpole, gullible and ferocious. She pursued him from one bride-chamber to the next, until he put on fresh brilliantine and exerted a remarkable spiritual force.

MRS. PRENTICE

This morning Mrs. Prentice showed me the walled garden of ancient roses. While we walked from bed to bed, there was an explosion at the docks and within minutes the air was white with dust, and the red roses white roses.

In her sandy garden she breeds nettles; from her crop she makes a sharp elixir that soothes sadness, prickly heat, and the itch. She says the earth is crowded with famished gods, each gnaws on an appropriate seed and rises as nettle, hollyhock, rose etc.

It is as though she took great pieces of ritual art out of the soil, treasure fragile and healthily obscene. She deals in perfumes that do not die, out of a ground buzzing with fountains. For a while there had been a gardener in charge called Stonepater, but she cleared his work away except for a small chapel for his memorial tablet. Even here she modified the altar into a fountain, the central jet of which took the place of the crucifix, and which refreshed the air in lieu of incense.

BY HIS OWN BOOTSTRAPS

I said to the middle-aged man sitting in the chair, you must prove your self-control. He said, put the blood-pressure cuff on. I did; his blood pressure was up, quite dangerously. That is because I hate doctors, he said, nothing personal. That is decidedly personal, since you have put yourself in my care, I said. Wait, he replied, and closed his eyes. There was a slight drop in the mercury. No, that is not quite enough, he said, before I could tell him the reading. With a careful gesture he put his forefingers in his two ears, sliding them in deep and steady. Now his blood-pressure was quite normal. He opened his eyes and smiled at me. There you are, then, he whispered. There was no point in replying, as he could not hear me, with those forefingers pressed in his ears, as though he were lifting his own skull on a pole.

MY HORSE

My horse gallops in his blazing visage and torrential mane. He pauses to drink at a stream. There is a rock clothed in its flowing water as transparent down to the bone as our ride has made my skin; and he, my horse, is always perfectly transparent to himself. There is a world of power beneath the ordinary water. But I must get on. I ride like a skeleton horseman through night, wind, perfume, through the balsamic forest. I arrive just at the moment when the uncle strikes the rock and the bride walks out of the cleft into this world and the mountain thunders. But before I can attend to her, I take mind that my horse is covered with clear sweat. I rub him down, promise him seven bright brass knobs to wear on his collar before I turn to the smiling lady.

A CARPENTER

This boy is a mystic, and wears the pigtail of a mystic. His experiences in the radiating cancer-wards have rendered him childless, but a sweet smell seeps from his exquisite joining and carpentry, everywhere you go in his house you are standing on or are raftered by the justice of his joining; particularly when the kitchen warms with the cooking there is the faint underscent of forests. He has also been a shipwright. He is angry to have had cancer and its treatment which has destroyed his generations, but not bitter, for he survives. Having been so close to death, he is accustomed to deep consideration, as it might be planning a complex joint in wood, to compile a bookcase, to escalate a staircase. His house is crafted like a ship. He has grown a new body from his immune system, but his skin is sewn with the scars through which the old guts were extracted. He will look after you if you are dying; this he has done for the two grandfathers; he will build you a ship of death smelling of pine.

SOCK

A few gentlemen of limited stature were drinking brandy in the back bar. Rice honey was on sale, in threepenny jars. The womenfolk were working in the fish cellars. Along the street the smell of five hundred bedrooms lingered. 'I'm a blouse man myself,' the drinker confessed shyly. The jukebox was playing 'Thin Worms Sing Long Songs'. 'Water remains true to itself, even as spit or froth,' ruminated the barman, drawing a pint of Sock.

SALT ON THE MEADOW

When I smelt the salt on the meadow the magical spaces of the landscape opened to me and I knew where I was. The sisters passed as they pleased through nature, a pride of nudes. When they wished to imitate smoke, the women flapped their shirts. There were so many feathers in the Town Square that they blew across the street and piled up in the bus shelters and up the library steps like bookmarks for all the books. Later, the furnace letters of winking neon advertised the nightclub now held in the old lambing shed with its sequence of triangular unglazed window spaces in which the featherless pigeons roosted. The Grand Hotel was entirely dark under the shadow of the limestone cliff. I had been holding all the time a note written in my father's gossamer hand. Through the heavy patterned curtain the sandy path led again to the boy in the tree. The dawn through the window seemingly lighted from below, the distances dark.

BESTIAL SHADE

The candle she lit was so black the flame seemed to be burning at the end of its own shadow. I spent hours walking the frozen streets in my red boots and with Mozart burning my ears, my Walkman turned up high; I walked under the black yew shags and the high cold sun. The shadow of a bear fell across my path – it was the bestial shade of the prick-bush which would shine its glass all winter. In these mists of yin, in these domes of cloud, she sees palaces that are eternal. One of the magicians, Mr. Priestman, is proudly taking his tooth home. The cat stretched out to five times his usual length on the piano lid in the full morning sun, his fur smelt like a scorching iron.

BEAUCOUP POISON

They have beaucoup poison – nose-candy, or cocaine -- did I say cockaigne? And music to go with it, produced by stroking catgut gently with the cut-off heads of whisky bottles. The TV is a jumping light like a ghost in a bottle. There are grey dust-kittens under the washing-machine, the following legend nailed to its front: 'And he answered and spake unto those that stood before him, saying, take away the filthy garments from him. And unto him he said, Behold, I have caused thine iniquity to pass from thee.' The starry night smelt of star-jasmine. Near the bonfire you could feel the hair in your nose getting crisp. To meet them again after so long, their child-faces all worn away.

HIS IDEA OF GLORY

Huge white clouds blown up into the sky by gathering thunder.

Flames breaking out of the yellowish coils of smoke of the bonfire lit in the forest clearing by the well.

The undertaker walking uphill with blue crepe tied around his top hat – 'His idea of glory,' somebody remarks.

I have put on my father's old Home Guard uniform and am standing in bright dawn light and I welcome the rain with a curtsey and with 'Good morning, my lady'.

'One would have thought the deep to be frosted and hoary, yet from the cliff the sea does indeed boil like a pot,' somebody quotes.

The well is still visible as a marshy pool by the ruins of the cottage.

She lived solely for forty years on the milk of a single cow.

Cornwall has the elixir of youth and the elixir of age, and delivers both equally.

BABY

The lusty lips of the immense baby spoke and said: 'We unconsciously imitate those we love. I have an unconscious only, as yet,' says the babe, 'where is my father now?' Unconsciously imitating himself as his father he went out to purchase a pint or two of soul-glue at the innocence-shop, and it was there that he met the white dress of Sister Eugenix. Being the son of his father, he had obtained a legacy of lilac-fields and coffee-shops, so he could afford to take her out. Her blinding white dress was like a cinema-screen, and when the show started he said to himself, as a father to a son, 'You can afford to relax, just a little.' She was certain he was ready for it, and, sure enough, when he looked again his longing for his father had turned into a sun-bleached wooden statue standing in a garden among lilacs – sunbleached wood as pale as any ghost, with its ancient thousands of wormholes like burrowing tears shed that had not yet erased the image, not quite yet. So he buried his head in her skirts and shed a few more wormholes under her auspices.

GUEST FATHER

What but the menstruation stretches out the rooms and gives pleasure in their every corner? Something about sewing with silk dreamed in the radiance of the menstrual smell. The second man rode in on the back of the Vesper Scooter, his hands folded behind him like an ice-skater, after Mrs. Prentice had shown him her garden of ancient roses. The barrels in the old winery are alive, they glisten, foam, belch, they smell of vinegar and spirits and dead leaves. I wanted to shout aloud that more, much more than we thought was alive, but then he started speaking in his duty-voice, annoyed with his wife – Moses was very badly possessed by the Mother of Colours – but then from the forest came an odour of immense cedar. At this he was again the Guest Father, double-soled in the whole play of his musculature and his repertory of glances. He looked down and snatched the periwinkle from his buttonhole; it was the flower of death with which the condemned were garlanded on their way to the gallows. There were explosions far off, and the two rivers became white with rock-dust.

SPLENDOUR

Her green skirts swirling like a great inner surface, the pearls shining in the water, the shirt glowing, the pearls glowing, and she in trance. The Almighty has plunged women into a sea of splendour. Her vulva like unto the footprint of a gazelle on the sands of the desert. And on the other hand she told him his skin was as soft and silky as though he wore an invisible nightie. He smelt the starlight and the bedrock and the perfume on the moon. Is that not splendour? she enquired. Unless amber be warmed and manipulated it retains its aroma within; woman is just such a creature that will yield its fragrance only when rubbed by the hands. They mixed their passion-loaded spittle and drank it together. She drew closer to the window, as the perfumes of the garden stored moonlight and released it again in strange waverings and shinings that were almost visible.

SLEEVE ANGELS

He likes that dress. Though it is so deep, it is barely a dress. It is threaded perfume. The man wore blue woollen armour, even in the scalding light. He spoke from between terraced houses of ivory. She who declared unto man what is his thought undid another button. If you don't like my peaches, why do you shake my tree? So he sent his hawklike claws among the tendrils. The dust was heavier than the silt in an Egyptian cistern. Outside their rooms were concrete bridges the colour of raw sausage. He changed into a traditional style robe with hood and angel sleeves in case she wanted to admire his magic touch.

HIS DOOM

His doom was to live famished. The house was in the Badlands. You could hear the ceilings, the drone of the high ceilings. She came in in freshly-dyed silver boots, and stripped down to a facetiously-pretty undergarment. Despite his distress, such men of the art have a two-sided skin. We shall not detail except to say that the next vivid trident lit the aperture with an unearthly brutality. Afterwards, she put on a welded hat and a pencil skirt. She remembered the pilot turning his head in the shining cockpit. That was a birth memory; could it be the same son who had gone into the local and ordered a Top Row? It was the crowning straw. She spoke of the nice warm flat that was destroying her gradually. How could they transform the Badlands? His famished doom: cause or symptom? It was their duty not to expel it upon the land, as by chat shows, news summaries, etc.

POEMS

I.

The miners in the tunnels under the Atlantic stopped work and listened to the great boulders above rolling over the seabed.

II.

The gull crying to the great tune, which is the storm coming.

III.

The tree lives inside its wooden fortress and the cherry-blossom bursts out of the keep like banqueting light.

IV.

Don't be shy about death, be an old man interested in it, like a virgin interested in sex.

V.

To die, or to become invisible.

VI.

His father dies, the son becomes more visible. He is the personification of death to the new generation. Because he has an invisible father, they are deferential to him, and he may well grow a beard at this point.

VII.

Can his father hear the rumbling of the boulder? Does he banquet with the light? Is he self-sufficient like the moon, mistress of self-propulsion?

VIII.

Come into the old man's house before he leaves for ever. The air is cologned with happier drinking-days, a fine Beaune reddened and tarred with age.

IX.

Age is the only smell left after he leaves. Except for the smells of the waterlilies meditating in the garden pond. That is an ageless smell.

X.

I am breathing rather fast in this house of his papers. Into what word has the air stilled itself in the chambers of his skull?

XI.

His darkened emission compares with my lighted one.

XII.

I am shaken. I ask for a cup of tea. But it is his voice I hear. My tongue has his taste. The tea tastes of a matured tree.

XIII.

'Wisdom hath built herself a house, which if any man enter in, he shall be saved, and find pastures' (Aurora Consurgens, Parable 5). But this home must be sold, having been cleaned of the effluvia of his last days, out of the curtains, out of the carpets, out of the paintwork. We scrub and scrub until there is only a clean ghost-house left, with no occupant.

XIV.

The bite-marks in the red apple turn it into a skull, slowly browning. Many old people have a post-mortem appearance. Is this his ghost, or have I dreamed of his death? Is he still dead when I awake?

XV.

'Beware lest the vinegar be turned unto smoke...' How deep her clothing is, surrounded with variety. We had a wonderful Sunday walk by a new path to Maenporth, some days after the death. As we passed a cottage-ruin that had extraordinarily thick walls, I said that I wished I could live in such fabric, in the walls as well as the passageways.

GLACIER MOTHER

Glacier Mother in silver, thundering, unloading iceberg daughters on the black water.

He was angered at the suggestion that he ferry the living across the dark water.

Some peculiarities of the foliage astonished him. And he gasped at the flowers and lessons of the thorn. 'What is the name of these woods?' he asked. 'Tell me!' he begged. 'I have been touching palaces in the dark.'

He counts but not in numbers. he is strengthened by the gravity of the gardeneress. He has the roar of prayer in his voice. The obedient great lilac folios open to him, under the broad grey bands of cloud that are the wave-crests to the wind, the boundless mazes wandering on into solace. The climax of it would be falling into the pond and thereby becoming another kind of creature.

There was no end to the imagery of the garden. In autumn it was beginning to resemble the skin of an infinite snake casting off and full of confused noises and voices.

She had asked the price at the place of entrance, paid, and entered the labyrinth, liking its shadiness. The deep pit of his kiss full of the imagery of the garden awaited her. She had become merely a woman with long hair cutting a field of onions – this was her usufruct. Now the meanings rose around her. The kiss created a fine but eerie mist, strangely veiled and shadowed. They ate the small flat cakes, the hyacinth a mere comma at the heart of its oniony lair.

AUTOBIOGRAPHY

I.

I am keeping a diary which is curiously composed. There appears to be oil in it and pebbles and it is cool. It is an autobiography which is also cool stones.

II.

There is an old-fashioned coalman unloading his horse-drawn cart which has stopped outside our house. He is wearing a leather tabard and a sack on his head which is split along one side to make a kind of cowl. He pulls open a flanged trapdoor set in the base of the house, allowing sun into the cool cellar. The stones he pours from his sacks are cool but black until in the fire they give off their milliard millenial warmth, returned sunshine.

III.

I declare my purpose of exploring my dens, to discover the power that quickens them. I descend the coal-cellar stairs and find that room blazing with sunshine, and black oily stones pour through the sunlight aperture or hatch. They pile up into a scree of black solid light shining in the sunlight. The rough stone walls of this den are layered with ruffles of coaldust. I sit cross-legged on the flagged stone floor and watch the pile of black stones grow, and its smell which is like pines and mud grows too. Why should a grown man be interested in cellars? The hatch thumps back and the space becomes as black as what half-fills it. If I close my eyelids it makes no difference to the lighting of this scene, which is absent.

IV.

My flesh is so young in the presence of this millenial being! Hearth-being and heart of the house. I reach out blindly and take a piece, a fruit of black solid forests. I fumble my way to the door and click open the latch and pictures once more appear. I look at the flat stone I have picked. There is the mark of a lily printed on its blackness. The fossil of a white lily, preserved in its black negative.

AB-TEENAGERS

I.

Teenagers haunting the disused cotton binderies at the eastern edge of town, washed out and ageless under the sodium glare. There was Gofer, an expert on weird matters and heavy duty inner space. There was S. for whom God wasn't quite good enough, S. Wolf, and his face was sleek, cocky and hedonistic. What did the S. stand for? That he leered. Then there was Rosy Blood, whose blouse opened like the title-page of a distinguished volume, and she the reading-stand. Sometimes it was illustrated with the frontispiece of a cameo brooch. Both boys supposed there was a body on the lines of the usual mothy-skinned female in there, but something about her body extinguished their recollections, and they never could remember, and this kept them faithful. Only, there again the blouse was, refreshed; should either one of them open that page again, and sleep? Sitting at the bar is the old fisherman. He looks into the soul of the weather, and beyond, into your soul. 'Oobie-joobie japonica, the naughty great thing,' crows Patrick, the last of the gang. He wears white moonboots. As they cross the carpark together, Rose in her great skirts like honorary bedsheets, they look like gnomes or pixies made taller by the night. That was the purpose, to look ab-human, so that their powers should come to them fresh, and not wearing parental faces. Patrick, whose father had recently died, guaranteed he would report when the dead man stopped whispering to him.

II.

Lots of the boys were dreaming of black fire, and bombs, and boobs: it was all part of the job of being a boy. 'Hello!' she said to anybody, 'Freaked to meet you!' and instantly he felt better. Then the incorrigible one who made actual bombs with cocoa tins and carbide came in. He called himself God's Liar and wore a big black badass hat. Our pretty subteen, who could not keep her eyes off his fly, mentioned that your shadow can get caught on holly-bushes if you walk through them, and if you pirouette through you could get absolutely shadowless – wouldn't that be neat! and squeezed him with her eyes. The other one, who wore perfume proudly as issuing from her budding chest, countered that she liked soldiers, but only peaceful ones. Her idea of womanhood was a military widow escorting her husband home on a ship: Smith, General, laid out in preservative oil, like a sardine with epaulettes; and she, discreetly amorous, catching a haughty subaltern offguard by prising off the lid and astonishing him with the mystery of a hale soldier gone away and departed and yet so perfectly present, in a light gold oil. Then all the rest of the people came in and there was no more talk as everybody settled down on the wide park benches to enjoy the moves in the gentle breeze that had been going on for billions of leaves, of green over green, the colour of lost emeralds.

ARTISTS IN CORNWALL

I.

The deep pit of his kiss by the easel. The air shines a little – the artists flock to Cornwall to paint invisible colours. His companion suckles her child who is strengthened by the gravity of his nurse. The roar of prayer is in his house and on his cliffs. A shadow falls across his canvas, he turns, it is a snow-white bullock; he smells its unmindful breath which is sweet as honey. He ate greedily but neatly. In the late sunbeams the cobwebs made bonfires of silk. In the moonlight, the avaricious fluency of birds, and the wink of lightning. What is constant, ever? he asked himself. What is constant is what cannot be repeated, he said, the sweetness of fresh water in the fountains where we met as friends. Partly so, she said; while we are alive, the constant thing is your body, my body, and those occasions when we see our bodies figured in outward things, as with those fountains, or this house, or the cliffs roaring with prayer. It is your sweetness which is constant, my friend, and thus I discover and acknowledge my own, and see it all around when out windows open.

II.

They sat thinking about the promoter with his shadowy money. The season was drawing the hyacinth like a wine from its oniony cellar. The foliage was already vibrating with bees. There was an aftertaste from the meditation, a newborn and elastic echo, yet also something that sank by its own weight to far depths. They open their eyes. The clouds shamble past. There is a young hare licking its paw near the roofed gate of the churchyard. The moon splits the air. They have built together an impalpable but totally real ancient city full of clues. Impalpable but visitable.

III.

'Nature… hath infinite beauties in herself, and all these she would gladly see beyond herself, which she cannot do without the Matter – for that is her glass. The least violence destroys it, enlightened with all the tinctures of the sun and stars.' He quotes. I have seen her. I have been her.

It moves here in shades and tiffanies – breath-assembly, dream concourse, immune system. This fine substance is the child of the elements. Their secret and famous Lunaria. 'It discovers itself and shines after night like pearl; the astral balsam which hath in it the whole anatomy of heaven. When it enters into the lower parts of this world, it overcasts them with a certain viridity, makes them break forth into flowers and presents us with something which is very like the Paradise we have lost.'

NOTES OF A GELSEMIUM PSYCHE

The pain in my jaw from the chafing of the new lower plate became noticeable after I woke from a beautiful sleep with many warm and coloured dreams. I had also been up on Pendennis Point in a harsh wind. The pain continued all night, fading in and out of the pleasant dreams, as though the pain were able to turn into mental pictures, and vice versa. This realisation gave me energy, and I was able to work well, finishing several jobs rapidly. I became tired at lunchtime, and the jaw swelled, so I went back to bed, and could not sleep, but sweated and turned. Did my energy come with the high pressure of the sunny morning, and the tiredness and painful jaw with the swirling and massive thunderous inky clouds out of the north-west that overcame the fine weather? I have often noticed that such a cloudscape which makes me unable to rest arrives after a particular exhilaration when I am at my peak – a cold front travelling after a warm front, or perhaps the electrical exhilaration of the storm's penumbra, which has an energy to it, while its nucleus is deadening and confusing. I find this cruel – that when I feel so well that I think I must be doing something right, it is a prelude to dismay, depression, draining of energy. I think it is the electrostatic turmoil of the clouds, and the available evidence bears me out. Now the showers came in, and I felt the prickling of them with shooting pains as I tried to rest. This was because they came with the wind, which was active and disturbing. Often I feel the tension between earth and sky as a shower impends, with a sudden and almost sexual relaxation as the rain falls. No wonder the Chinese called the act of love 'The Clouds and the Rain'.

When I start to feel haunted, I know that the weather is about to change, or is changing. I become attentive to shadows. A dark cloth thrown over a chair startles me as I catch sight of it out of the corner of my eye. I think for a moment that the cat is streaking through the room as I turn to confirm the shadow. The knob of the newel post in the hall suddenly reminds me of a creamy skull of a child, and I almost *see* this. What is the weather doing? I look out of the window – that strange summer mist has gathered with its tension; I am not surprised; that high-pressure mist always gives abominable feelings, and its haunt has reached into my house. I wash my hands, a shadow comes up behind me. I will not look to see what it is behind me, though my back-hairs are prickling. I think that what is there is non-verbal input from my right brain. Once I was put on a 'mind-mirror' which is an electroencephalograph that shows the brainwaves of both hemispheres simultaneously. Mine showed a pattern like a pair of beating wings, both sides were contributing their quota. Then they rounded, these wings, into an egg shape. So I am getting input from both sides; the instrument confirms this.

Though the fluctuations of mental and physical energy are sometimes difficult to bear calmly, I am in a strange way content with such happenings. They are images of events that I have tried to understand and to evolve with as a writer. What I fear, though, is the 'flu, which for me is sheer deadness with no changes for as long as it lasts, restlessness, insomnia, pain. I am very glad to have the Gelsemium picture, which means, I assume, that with this remedy I am not likely to get so stuck in these weather-associated depressions, but can move and change as is demanded of me. How often had I seen without understanding: the great cloud over Leeds when I lived on the hills above it, that radiated dismal feelings that made me want to run far away; the dreams of being grounds by loose cobbles in a machine like an electrical castle as the great Falmouth hailstorms passed overhead; and that experience when I first came to Falmouth and stood on the jetty at Flushing, and out of a clear and sunny sky it was as though a troop of demonic horsemen wheeled in the sky and turned round to attack me with themselves, successions of dark thoughts and draining emotion as they impalpably crashed into me.

I have tried to keep my doors open. I am sure that allopathic treatment would close them, so I would at no time seek relief from the mechanical medicines. I have kept a dream journal in great detail for more than twenty years. It is this, and the disciplines of writing poetry, that have provided me with images whose energies may interact with me instead of creating inarticulate fear and disturbance. Thus I have discovered other influences than weather are abroad, which are gentler yet not unconnected with the weather patterns. For instance, I dream into the poet Shuttle's menstrual cycle, which is a kind of household weather, and I have dreams which relate to the events of her cycle-day. I dream of treasures put away carefully at the receding threshold of her menstruation, as the tide of blood ebbs; of wonderful rounded treasures at her ovulation: globes, bubbles, fruit, round tables; of terrible deaths at her late luteal phase, when the ovum is breaking up and giving off its last energies, and yet the pregnancy hormone, progesterone, is at its peak, potential pregnancy fighting its opposite; of electricity and fire during her advancing premenstrual threshold; of blood and life and mental fertility during her bleeding. We have been able to contribute something to the knowledge of these real and ignored influences on human lives, and in this the Gelsemium personality has made its contributions.

III. IN THE BLACK MIRROR

CARN BRAE IN THE BLACK MIRROR

The houses are the forms and volumes carved out of space-time by the necessary routines of the people, the underworld by the lawful designs of water and rock.

As I pass this way in the dark, I can feel the chill of the formal ancient pend or vaulted gateway arching over me, an arch which completes itself into a circle in the sub-underworld beneath my feet.

In the warm room she remarks on my erection and denies that there need be squalor or unwholesomeness in the low rite.

Her eyes fell open like the trapdoors called 'vampires' in the old theatre which, like Cornwall, is hollow under its boards, while we, actorish, dwell on its surface.

There is a London Coliseum of galleries and circuses, and a Paris Opera beneath the green hills, which are great halls, meadows honeycombed with vents, towns whose staircases descend beneath their cellars and whose attics open on their subterranean beaches.

What tides march to and fro in these low thoroughfares playing the great Town hall organs underground?

There is the earth's anguish as it is mined and the chambers where an echo never dies away completely, never truly stops, but gathers and rolls into other resonant echoes until with a great shout a mineshaft collapses in steam and dust.

The echo of this collapse travels underground out of the county until it meets the great batholith of Dartmoor, which bounces it back. There are return echoes from the granite inclusion south, called the Scilly Isles.

Our dreams are full of the interesting squalor of these pits redeemed by their reverberations.

I suggest to her that the low rite would be even more wholesome if performed a hundred feet underground.

All holes in the earth or under it are interesting, so on the brink of that mineshaft she comments on her interior hard-on excited by the depth and smell of water.

Naturally I open my trousers in homage to this great yoni.

The woman interposes her humanity and it seems to us that we travel in the mines as the indigenous tides and echoes do.

'You have one mother of a boner,' she says to me. 'And you have a record-breaking excavation,' I remark as her man-engine plumbs our depths.

WELSH HILLS IN THE BLACK MIRROR

I.

A mutual vast fuck of limestone and water. It has been going on for ever; we stand in its presence. This cliff is full of churches turned inside-out; they pour out a landscape of noise shaped by these inwards. The interior torrents are their microseisms of the area. The water is rolling fat with its stone. It is an elixir which leaves behind architecture. The water brings everything it has seen into these caverns and deposits it there.

II.

The caverns are the world's nostril with its rubble and lofty turbinals. There is the stone-carving smell of a sculptor's studio as soon as you get your head in there. The smell of the sculptor's breath in the rush of his nostril. Where is the sculptor? Why is he invisible? He is not. He is the shine on the walls, reflecting like moonlight to the torches, and you may see him roll across your palms in this small pursy water-drop. Water through rock generates birdsong in certain registers of the dripping steps, soul-sound winds down the thin spires, monstrous rosettes are linked by the vibration of gondoliers' bridges. Did I say 'he'? The river-water of the foothills having passed through these processes warbles in the sunlight meadows; the water still plunged in the caverns shouts down its precipices, black on black.

III.

Outside, on the hillslopes, the may-trees heavy with odorous power, Persephone-power, the core of the breeze, her cunny smell in the shockheaded blooms. Before, after and during the May, her one-to-the-nth power of fingers wriggling through the limestone as she plays the porous keyboards, organ music played by work done in the stone. The limewater covers the stone with stone, the silence of the cliffs is subsonic music. It is as one comes in under the tabernacle of a tree, there is never less than faint music in the ear's porches.

IV.

The mountains as full of apartments, bathrooms and wet ballrooms as all the hotels in Cardiff put together. 'A wedding in Wales?' A true wedding would be in these caverns, whose insides are dressed in bridal limestone appliqué already. A bridal deep within the lacy Bride, deep within Wales, among the subsonic organs and the bird-like chirping of water in shining aviaries and veils, married inside the vast Bride, married in one of her dresses of dresses; the celebrants enter and are clothed with the interior of the hills.

V.

St. Paul's in London is a cave-system of altars and painted caverns. Within this Welsh hill is a cave-system astronomically larger than St. Paul's. There are a thousand altars shining with darkness. Small tightly-cinctured sinkholes that are very marshy give ingress through the mud. I wallow in this mud to reach my inner church, which is full of darkness until I bring my torches looking for its core. These muddy ingresses bestow their unctions so that one is being married into mud before one is re-married in these dripping robes in the inner cathedral; or the sump or syphon is a vestry.

VI.

Landscape stretching out within landscape, Persephone-power of union; every reedy marsh on this hill has its ingress, though many are too strait for the adult human body. These are the fortifications of shakeholes and seasonal lakes; access can vary from easy to moderately difficult to perilous lock-systems and syphons requiring diving-equipment. The diver raises his head, and with his head his lamp, out through the eclipsed dark of the inner space that has not tasted light in a million years. The underground lake laps the light up. My dowsing body knew beforehand the inner spaces of these hills that rang like stone bells to one who can best hear in the dark. I sought the inner space in many small marshes until I found the way in, beneath the skin.

VII.

The cliffs are so high up they feel deep down. Limestone caves merge into bubble-caves of lava that rolled down on this forest which is preserved intaglio on these walls. The patient delving of the cliffs like a measureless fuck of water with rock; the cunt grows greater with the prolonged gentle fucking. Outside, clouds like daisy-chains laid along the wind in the passionately blue sky.

CORNISH HILLS IN THE BLACK MIRROR

Lumps of sulphur, like the Chinese oracle wrapped in yellow silk. Knowledge and anticipation. The dark glass cases in the museum alight with yellow sulphur-patches. Certain sunny gardens of crystal sulphur have been retired to these shelves of the Geological Museum. I read the cards and admire the Latin but watch for the life of these crystals lighting up my own interior museum. Many of the powers that transmit energy from underground, controlling our ways, rest here in palpable colourful specimens. The great nether bedrooms radiating post-coital peace. Flaming tar-balls skim across the surface of clear underground lakes. Their shores are quivering quilts of mud, of shivering sand. The roomy Venusbergs, the ballrooms, sumps, latrines, halls, galleries, bedrooms – all stained in gorgeous swatches of ore, sometimes approaching the condition of landscape-tapestry. Her great copper bedrooms, the mile-long bedrooms of Venus. Staircases of quartz climbing to kitchens coloured like beetroot with iron ore; wet tin ore silvering precipices. All the emanations concentrated and visible at last. Marshalling yards of recurrent caves. These caves travelling around unseen inside the hills, like escalators and lifts that can move in any direction. Think of the shed of an alchemist: and the passageways of vapour between the massive units of equipment – that is the mountain with its caves winding, the gigantic alembics that distil and redistil the lime-freighted water and release it at last in laddering torrents out of sump-holes in sunny precipices, containing in liquid form the masonry and design of many cathedrals that will be laid down elsewhere as it sinks hollowing out the ground for its vaulted crypts. Indeed, the alchemist has become his work, only his beards remain – they rouse themselves in any piece of water that begins to move, that leaps off a rock in its dive. He is sheer play, which it was his purpose to become. He presides everywhere, transmitting his messages imprinted in his substance by the planets and the higher minerals which transduce the planetary influences and those of the stars, as do the gemstones' crystal points. As below, so above; he seeks to make a perfect model of the universe out of rocks and ores down below, so that the earth shall resonate the constellations in perfect rhythm.

It began with the mining which created an underground city as vast as the county. The magicians took over from the miners, and certain alchemists dissolved themselves into the rock, singing. You can see the crystal pattern of Merlin's beard inlaid on the wall of his esplumeor in the cave at Tintagel, the birth-cave where the baby Arthur was found. Thus the world began to alter in its own way and become intelligible in Latin, however otherwise it might appear. There is praise below the rocks under the turf and many churches as they sing move up and down their roads and hills inside the rock, inside the black mountain with its floors moving up and down with the doors opening and shutting like the true and veritable original of the ghost-house, with the heads popping out of the secret panelling. The buses and charabangs driving to the ghost-house under the hill are churches on the move. The clouds above whiten with ice as they rise like refrigerated lifts, or descend, blushing with the warm rain that enters the ghost-house like fresh legions through innumerable pores. On certain days, every object whether aboveground or below it becomes a fountain of ghost.

THEIR COWS AND THEMSELVES

The saliva and wine of all trees, flowers and plants. The gale is like a perfumed cannon fired. As the alighting bird touched it, a sheath of water fell off the telephone wire. When two leafcutting ants meet they stop and exchange information via their saliva, and this can include complex messages regarding food sources, etc. The wine of his jaws. Hers. Gustatory conjuring... When the Moon is dark it comes to earth and waits for you in the place of sacrifices. If you insulate the houses of a city, that city is cooler than if you grew a forest there. A city that does not warm the air at night is a piece of land that cools faster after the sun goes down, forming whirling cliffs of air, tight vortical effects, wind-demons and whirlwinds such as those that plucked the branches away in Budoc Wood, while the sea holds its heat and projects eroding warm air into the invisible massifs, which tumble. None of this happens in the warm city built on the shores of a warm sea; there is an easier balance, there is less crime. But more methane, yes; the heat of the city and the bodies of the millions who inhabit it also change the weather, like the rainmakers of old. The vast defiles of methane herd into the sky, the carbon dioxide of their lungs and vehicles, the methane of their gas-supplies, their cows, their selves.

MASER TALK

'Thus, there is an uncanny pulse from the female wing-beat...'

The Black Goddess Chapter II

I.

Our atmosphere of gases soaks up energy until it can hold no more, so heavy it is with power; it starts beating with a coherent pulse like a drumbeat, shedding subvisible light on the occasion, including human infra-red, which lights up our emotions; the envelope of gases in this sickroom is charged up by our racing pulses, and his failing one. I hear his heart stop. The lub-a-dub is succeeded by silence (for we too must hold our breath, lest it escape with his), then by a cool rushing like rain shed in rhythmic waves. This torrent, fading, is the sound the conscious mind and the unconscious make when they rush together and slide sideways into a new dimension which has a different pulse.

II.

As if we were surrounded by spirits with one queenly heartbeat, which we are.

III.

It is a regal dress for in its excited state it soaks up radiation from everywhere and alters its pulse accordingly. Our bodies generate this sheath of gases which is a robe embroidered with resonances representing planets, and sparking with the constellations. The silks of queens would be a model of it, were they woven in transistor brocades. It sees by radio, this charged gas, this universal and fluid aerial, this wildfire that is dry water not wetting a finger.

IV.

Thus the clitoral finger brings down star-jelly by maser. In the secret garden upstairs the stars shine down through the unbroken ceiling and cannot be observed except through the observatory skin with its micro-climate broadcasting, like a radar, human oscillation. This is as figured as the star-dome itself, depending on the accuracy of the fingering, and

these high frequencies the human slows to audible ecstatic speech. The
bodies spread around them a dark lake in which, with stillness, the stars
appear, and the light of them in these depths is that of an unseen colour
out of space, which, nevertheless, can be discussed.

V.

Thus a sudden roseknotgarden in the bedroom. I pad my way through
the labyrinth to its centre. As we touch mutually our quick we open
observatories to the sky, which signal, as described. The winds of space
blow through this room, they are perfumed with energies that are busily
relating. Our bodies drink them, because we are thirsty.

VI.

Moths fur the windows of the house, muffled two-storey retort. Even
beasts so frail as these are winged keys to the invisible, heavy-winged seals
on the second senses. Her reclining figure in violin-shape pulsates as
though the skin were all moth and myrrh.

VII.

Her body was a triumphant army marching. All the soldiers wore the
same pink shirt. The sounds she made were these: a swarm of bees; a
waterfall; the humming of telephone wires; the ringing of a bell; the
roaring of the sea; the rustling of tiny silver chains; flute notes; shrill, high
whistling; the sound of a drum echoed by distant thunder.

VIII.

But then I noticed that all bodies made this sound. It was the sound
of the crossed laths of the window. No doubt the ruby-blooded toad,
nightingale of the mud, made this noise, as did the river pouring by; the
silence certainly made this sound, the body of the silence.

IX.

Then I noticed that the silence was simply the valley of the pulse, and
that the sequence of events was this: thunder stirred in the earth and leapt
out of it in lightning, creating a mighty wind which caused a cloudburst

of rain. That immense shower then produced the valley of itself – a silence clearing the sky in which the sun and the moon came out, glittering on the lake and warming its fertility within the mountain of silence; then thunder rumbled again within its hinterlands.

THE CRYSTALLISATION PROCESS

The crystallisation process is symbolised by the building of the treasure-house by two poor labourers. They are in rags, but these are clean rags. The rich alchemist who has not gained his riches by alchemy strolls by. What is that celestial perfume? It accompanies the crystallisation and formation of the wonder-working stone. But the tower is empty and as yet unroofed, like a vast chimney. Is this smell a property of the building-stones, white granite from Penryn? His labourers who earn two coins a day each, slowly secure the capstone, and the shaft falls dark. The wonderful smell is stronger now. The rich man falls to his knees and appears to be praying, but he is sniffing the planks of the floor, wondering if the smell comes up from the earthen foundations; perhaps some jasmine stealthily growing in a few chinks of sunlight let through into the dark cellar. The labourers are descending their ladder, which they have had to hire for one coin. They are anxious to get it back by sundown. The rich alchemist gets to his feet and fumbles for their fee. As the money passes he understands that the wonderful smell they have bestowed on his useless treasure-house is the natural sweat of their building it.

CONFESSION OF THE BLOOD-HOLDER

There was a touch of amber in the cat's coat and a grin on the bottle of poison. Then the clouds started coming apart at the seams. The dead woman's wardrobe, the jewelry had to be removed from the collars. His father snoozed under a sheet of pale cream cloth; his own tears were falling freely in the folds of his mother's dresses, one of which father had made into a shroud, and waxed for his cere-cloth. My brother still lies there in the coffin as among petticoats, his cold lip lifted, his dry chipped teeth, his eyes tightly closed. His buttons broke open and let out insects which started to devour him, they swarmed like a personal torrent of the tide of all the white buttons in the world breathing inset on their shirt-fronts; as he was not breathing they multiplied and overflowed the coffin. After they had gone I went quietly to the coffin to peer in. Nothing rested on the white petticoat-satin. His clothes were neatly folded on the coffin-lid. Secular miracles! So I became a Franciscan. I soon started to fly. My sandals were squeaky as the songs of young frogs. The great test-tube containing the Holy Blood was mounted in two heavy gold cornices. As I held it high over my head it glistened and flickered in all the assemblages of lights, and a shout went up – it flowed, it was alive! A Franciscan, called Father.

FROM THE ANNOTATIONS OF P. PEDROSTONE

He had attempted to pull the mountain over his head by building the big stone house. It had a ghost in every room, a waterfall in the garden, caves and images and ponds and streams and a path called 'Alchemist's Walk' twining through the herb-gardens and orchards. On this path the jealous dead were wont to walk like a frost at night. I recall screwing with X all day in the garden room of this house. Grandfather's old radio was turned on, and made a twangling like a stack of harps. The covers shuffled off and we fell into sleep like fatalists. I woke some time later, the radio voice was saying '…the truth is in thy hands…'. I slept again, and woke to hear a different voice saying '…the great surprise was for a sauropod to be able to chase its food at all…'. X told me that was nonsense, the latter voice had been giving a talk on the beauty of the clitoris, particularly its aura, which manifested as a shimmering rainbow or a peacock's tail. 'Put your ear to my cunt and hear its cry,' she fondly urged.

RICHMOND PARK IN THE BLACK MIRROR

I.

The royal forest seemed to be a copy of the panelled room, but then we came out of the dark canopies into the green clearing. Smoke from the chimneys of Ham House packed into the low cloud, like foothills to those mountains. She took the sampler out of her bag and showed it to me. It stated in embroidery: 'Take comfort; thou wouldst not be seeking me, hadst thou not already found me', and on its back the stiff piece of cloth bore a stain on it like the face of a baby.

II.

The tourbillions of small rain pausing along the royal avenues and coachways, tall white king or the ghosts of kings, towering over the trees, slowly spinning. Deer run through the wet park, the small rain saddles them, and rides, like the imprint of the wet knees of kings. The deer run, scattering rainbows; they rest in their shining packs, reclining in the downpour; as we approach them, they turn their heads like one bush; out of the leader's brow, a tree branches, full of bright wet, scattering as he turns.

III.

The black girl's shuddah eyes look at me through the cadillac's opera window, they are as large as the bowls of spoons, her mouth shimmers as with his seed, they are driving through the forest where the white girl showed me the sampler, the whole forest is shimmering with dew; gifts of dew pour from the sky and stand in their proportion wherever one looks, even inside the great car proportion is extracted by the tourbillions of the cassette player, as the limousine sweeps by like an orchestra.

STORIES

The mines are resting now, recuperating their ores. Then they will be reborn. Feed the crystal with blood once a fortnight. After drinking, it will fall into a peaceful sleep. As we bake bread, so we will smelt metals. But the tin ore should be extracted without the mine's knowledge. An angel once appeared to a smith who had hitherto fed his furnace with wood and showed him a glistening black door leading through a coal-seam into an anthracite gallery. Again, a certain saint noticed the metal oozing from the stones of his hearth and thus learnt smelting. There was an electrical white lady who saved miners when her presence whizzing through the tunnels announced a strain building up in the rocks. So the Bakitara smith treats the anvil like a bride – as they carry it into the house they sing as though for a nuptial procession; the smith sprinkles it with water in order that it may beget many children, echoing with his blows. Ores have to be stalked, like game. The stones of light are stalked through the underground darkness. And the sacred smiths work the meteorite with silex hammers: the pure metal that arrives on the earth with a trail like an unsheathed sword.

THE LABORATORY OF FILTH

I.

I would have seen with my enlarged and numerous senses the blood on the apron. The newborn hugged and wrapped in a hairy blanket. The white rubberoid apron, or gray, the uniform collar above, the white rim, denoting Nurse of the Circumcision. The skin on fire with the birth and the circumcision instantly after, the touch and the word of God in the cut creating a particle of self in that great furnace of the skin raw from having been stripped from the womb. Last week in my ritual I was both midwife and child, seeing my condition in the mirror, my jersey higher than usual in the neck like an apron. I saw myself: somebody who has been working with birth fluids. Who was drenched in his birth. Fit. Afterwards, in bed, in old style, many orgasms. Exchange of elixirs. Distillation of elixirs while sleeping. God many-formed in the alembics.

II.

A miner, coated with my rich ores. The filth transmits its wonder-energy to the skin, its rainbow of oils into the skin, the ritual distils the wonder-energy into the skin, like a poultice which itself can later be discarded. The saint considers the pure metal oozing out of the rocks of which his hearth is made. The tin-streamers welcoming the ringing saint-metal. 'The borderline patient has a core of madness that must be uncovered if successful treatment is to be achieved... This true self might be represented as a child living in filth...' I quote from Swartz-Salant. The Queen of it all is also gilded sordidly with her own fluids and faeces and as the skin of her, which is her, rolls off the babe, the indigo skin of her child respires, blushes through turquoise to gold, and then the vernix should be rubbed in.

WET FACES

The wet faces of the clouds above, and these woods are thickly stoked with fiery wild pigs. The buoyant city of waters has descended into the canopy of the forest. I encounter a large mud-puddle ragged as a psychologist's inkblot in the middle of the path: I tend to experience hallucinations near mud or in its presence, like Persephone-power from an underworld mirror. A rush of wild piggery stampedes across my path, writing a bible of mud odorous with their droppings, hackles of steam rising along their hot spines, shouldering the slim treetrunks. The trees respond with showers of pure dew that blot out certain characters that the hoof parteth, being themselves heavy with odorous power.

MALVERN IN THE BLACK MIRROR

Malvern mist made of Malvern water – Langland drank, and saw his poem. A look of visionary selfishness, a criminal look. The motion-sensitive lights. The snowshine moved like trembling water about the furniture among fruits and vessels. I can hear the sun creaking the roof. Gloves and purses made out of shell-silk, the byssal threads of the Noble Pen Shell. The great boa feather mistaken for the skeleton of a snake. A piece of a medieval midden rich and hard as mahogany he used as his pillow for dreams. A note, written in her father's gossamer hand, spiderly. A fading green plot of grass at the cemetery where the ashes are cast. They are killing the grass. Cast them in the long wild grass, not in the mown acre, cast them into the jaws of the tigerish grass. The death-bed pillow, manure-rich with sweat. Then he called for his hard dreaming pillow; the mists of Malvern were gathering. The tiers of pollen in the Alexandra garden, the smell in the air changed when the words of affection were spoken – it was not the words themselves, but the speaking of the words.

THE LIMESTONE CAT

(For N.R.)

There are certain waters which have the ability to give birth to stones, or to petrify. There was once this bird which splashed the water over its wings as it flew over Whitewell or Silverwell, and fell into the water as if Gorgonised; the small dark bird has grown within the well to a giant white dove, which is still growing. The mosses in such waters accumulate in massive white beards quantities of travertine, and indeed form the great dams of the Plitvice Lakes. One male visitor threw his hat on top of the wet rock; now the shining boulder is crowned with trilby stone. Strike this almost-transparent headstone with the old broomhandle provided and it will start to hum like a Tibetan bell; inside, vaguely shadowed, is a limestone cat poised over a pebble-mouse, the cat's savage gesture eternised; touch the rock and it will be like touching the electrified fur of the cat; water-paws reach out to hunt watermice at the boulder's base where the stream runs in a stone trough of its own devising. Visitors walk through a small garden full of encrusted animals and the life-sized models in stone of previous proprietors as it were snapshot in rock as they raise a cup of stone tea to their petrified lips.

DRESSED AS FOR A TAROT PACK

He is a poet who paints vibrant pictures in your imagination, creating a chamber of experiences with each poem, giving the reader an invitation to revel in all their five senses, sparked from a single word catalyst. *Dressed As For A Tarot Pack* is a fresh and highly evocative collection of new poetry, created by a talented author, deserving of more recognition. Peter Redgrove is an essential poet, gifted with sensuality, a self-confessed magician. *(Topical Books)* £4.99

THE LABORATORS

Peter Redgrove has been at work again (is he ever not?) in his laboratory of the human spirit, alchemising all sorts of matter into gold... In *The Laborators* the 'Reader in Water at the University of Rock' as he calls himself in 'Enterprise Scheme', shows once again the extraordinary fecundity of his imagination, images reproducing, dividing, proliferating with protean vitality. And he shows too that no one else has the same ability to deal in the weightiest and most elemental themes of birth, sex, nature and death with quite his lightness of touch. With his angels and spirits and depictions of all kinds of energy, Redgrove is as bold and wise as Blake, and breezier with it. *(Stand)* £6.50

ABYSSOPHONE

Streets ahead of anything else... is Peter Redgrove, one of Britain's greatest unconventional voices. Redgrove's work at first may seem surreal but there is no arbitrary imagery at work here. His ideas embrace Gaia, world-as-one-living organism, the Jungian vision of the soul and the myth and magic of women as the sensual organiser of the world. *Abyssophone* sees him returning to the small presses with a brilliant new Stride production while continuing his scientifically observed flight into the mesmeric realms of the unconscious. *(New Welsh Review)* £6.95

ORCHARD END

The new poems in Orchard End open up yet more magical vistas in Peter Redgrove's apparently limitless poetic house and grounds. His is a spiritual, richly imaginative and inventive art, dancing with imagery like a pond full of fish on a bright day, yet firmly based in the everyday, the here-and-now the author observes and science tries to explain. Redgrove is a shaman, a priest and healer, a seer in whose work what is all around us – dog, cat, chocolate, window, fog, sandwich – intimates a hidden, more abundant life. As always, water and liquid movement find him at his best, as in 'The Mortier Water Organ', with its snaking jets and inner fountains, or the puddles and bottled rain of 'Service', a poem beautiful in its sexuality and full of puckish joie de vivre.

All books are available, post free, from the publishers:
STRIDE, 11 SYLVAN ROAD, EXETER, DEVON EX4 6EW
(cheques payable to 'Stride' please)